Religious education

GLOSSARY OF TERMS

£4
ISBN 1 85838 041 3
First published 1994
© 1994 School Curriculum and Assessment Authority

Reproduction, storage, adaptation or translation in any form or by any means of this publication is prohibited without prior written permission of the publisher, or within the terms of licences issued by the Copyright Licensing Agency. Excerpts may be reproduced for the purposes of research, private study, criticism or review, or by education institutions solely for educational purposes without permission, providing full acknowledgement is given.

Printed in Great Britain

The School Curriculum and Assessment Authority is an exempt charity under the Charities Act 1960.

School Curriculum and Assessment Authority, Newcombe House, 45 Notting Hill Gate, London W11 3JB

Chairman: Sir Ron Dearing CB

RELIGIOUS EDUCATION: GLOSSARY OF TERMS

The glossary is a revision of *Religious Studies – A Glossary of Terms. GCSE* which was published by the School Examination Council (SEC) in 1986. With the publication of the model syllabuses for religious education, and the work involving the faith communities in Britain, it was felt to be an appropriate time for revision.

The glossary has been devised by the different faith communities to:

- give guidance to teachers on key words and their meanings within each religious tradition which appears within the model syllabuses and within GCSE and A Level syllabuses;
- try to reach some form of consensus on spellings. This is almost an impossible task, due to the problems of transliterating from one script to another, for example from Gurmukhi with 35 characters into the Roman script of 26 characters.

It is important for pupils to build up a working knowledge of key words and technical terms which are used within each religion, and which are therefore central to religious education.

It is hoped that publishers will take note of the work that has gone into the glossary which has had the full backing of religious traditions represented in the UK, so that all resources produced henceforth to support religious education, all new agreed syllabuses and religious studies exams will adopt the preferred form emphasised in bold within this document.

Words printed in red are themselves main entries and can be cross-referenced within this glossary. Literal translations into English are printed in *italics*.

Acknowledgements are due to:

- all those who produced the original SEC glossary which has been a firm foundation on which to build, especially the Religious Education Council of England and Wales;
- the faith communities and organisations consulted on the publication of the model syllabuses for religious education.

BUDDHISM GLOSSARY

As Buddhism spread throughout the East, it came to be expressed in many different languages. Terms in the Sanskrit and Pali of India are in most common use in the West, although Japanese and Tibetan terms also occur frequently. Pali is the language of the texts of the Theravada school, whilst Sanskrit is used for general Mahayana. Zen Buddhism uses terms expressed in Japanese, and Tibetan Buddhism, Tibetan. There is no preferred form. For convenience, Pali terms appear in bold except in cases where the Sanskrit or other alternative is the more usual form.

PALI	SANSKRIT	EXPLANATION
Abhidhamma	Abhidharma	*Further* or *higher teaching.* The philosophy and psychology of Buddhism in abstract, systematic form.
Abhidhamma Pitaka	Abhidharma Pitaka	This is the third of the three principal sections of the canon of basic scripture. It is a systematic, philosophical and psychological treatment of the teachings given in the Sutta Pitaka.
	Amitabha Amitayus	Also, Amida (Japanese). Buddhas having unlimited light and life respectively.
Anapanasati	Anapanasmrti	*Mindfulness of the breath.* The practice most usually associated with the development of concentration and calm, but also used in the training of Vipassana (insight).
Anatta	Anatman	*No self; no soul.* Insubstantiality; denial of a real or permanent self.
Anicca	Anitya	*Impermanence; transience.* Instability of all things, including the self.
Arahat, Arahant	Arhat	*Enlightened disciple.* The fourth and highest stage of Realisation recognised by the Theravada tradition. One whose mind is free from all greed, hatred and ignorance.
Asoka	Ashoka	Emperor of India in the 3rd century BCE.
Atta	Atman	*Self; soul.*
Bhikkhu	Bhikshu	Fully ordained Buddhist monk.
Bhikkhuni	Bhikshuni	Fully ordained Buddhist nun.
Bodhi Tree		The tree *(ficus religiosa)* under which the Buddha realised Enlightenment. It is known as the Tree of Wisdom.

Buddhism

PALI	SANSKRIT	EXPLANATION
Bodhisatta		*A Wisdom Being.* One intent on becoming, or destined to become, a Buddha. Gotama, before his Enlightenment as the historical Buddha.
	Bodhisattva	A being destined for Enlightenment, who postpones final attainment of Buddhahood in order to help living beings (see Mahayana).
Brahma Viharas		The four sublime states: loving kindness, compassion, sympathetic joy, and evenness of mind.
Buddha	Buddha	*Awakened* or *Enlightened One.*
Dalai Lama (Tibetan)		*Great Ocean.* Spiritual and temporal leader of the Tibetan people.
Dana	Dana	*Generosity; giving; gift.*
Dhamma	Dharma	*Universal law; ultimate truth.* The teachings of the Buddha. A key Buddhist term.
Dhammapada	Dharmapada	Famous scripture of 423 verses.
Dukkha	Duhkha	*Suffering; ill; unsatisfactoriness; imperfection.* The nature of existence according to the first Noble Truth.
Gompa (Tibetan)		Monastery; place of meditation.
Gotama	Gautama	Family name of the Buddha.
Jataka		*Birth story.* Accounts of the previous lives of the Buddha.
Jhana	Dhyana	Also Ch'an (Chinese) and Zen (Japanese). Advanced meditation.
Kamma	Karma	*Action.* Intentional actions that affect one's circumstances in this and future lives. The Buddha's insistence that the effect depends on volition marks the Buddhist treatment of kamma as different from the Hindu understanding of karma.
Karuna	Karuna	*Compassion.*
Kesa (Japanese)		The robe of a Buddhist monk, nun, or priest.
Khandha	Skandha	*Heap; aggregate.* The Five Khandhas together make up the 'person' (form, feeling, perception, mental formation and consciousness).

Buddhism

PALI	SANSKRIT	EXPLANATION
Khanti	Kshanti	*Patience; forbearance.*
Kilesa	Klesa	Mental defilement or fire, such as greed, hatred or ignorance.
Koan (Japanese)		A technical term used in Zen Buddhism referring to enigmatic or paradoxical questions used to develop intuition. Also refers to religious problems encountered in daily life.
Kwan-yin (Chinese)		Also, Kannon (Japanese). Bodhisattva of Compassion, depicted in female form. Identified with Bodhisattva Avalokitesvara.
Lama (Tibetan)		*Teacher,* or one who is revered.
	Lotus Sutra	A scripture of major importance to various schools within the Mahayana tradition. It describes the virtues of the Bodhisattva, and emphasises that all sentient beings possess Buddha-nature and can attain Enlightenment (Nirvana).
Magga	**Marga**	*Path,* leading to cessation of suffering. The fourth Noble Truth.
	Mahayana	*Great Way* or *Vehicle.* Teachings that spread from India into Tibet, parts of Asia and the Far East, characterised by the Bodhisattva Ideal and the prominence given to the development of both compassion and wisdom.
Mala		Also, Juzu (Japanese). String of 108 beads used in Buddhist practice (like a rosary).
Metta	Maitri	*Loving kindness.* A pure love which is neither grasping nor possessive.
Metta Sutta		Buddhist scripture which describes the nature of loving kindness.
Metteya	Maitreya	One who has the nature of loving kindness. Name of the future Buddha.
Mudda	**Mudra**	Ritual gesture, as illustrated by the hands of Buddha images.
Mudita	Mudita	*Sympathetic joy.* Welcoming the good fortune of others.
Nibbana	**Nirvana**	*Blowing out* of the fires of greed, hatred and ignorance, and the state of secure perfect peace that follows. A key Buddhist term.
Nirodha	Nirodha	*Cessation* (of suffering). The third Noble Truth.

Buddhism

PALI	SANSKRIT	EXPLANATION
Panna	Prajna	*Wisdom.* Understanding the true nature of things.
Parami	Paramita	A perfection or virtue. One of the six or ten perfections necessary for the attainment of Buddhahood.
Parinibbana	Parinirvana	Final and complete nirvana reached at the passing away of a Buddha.
Patimokkha	Pratimoksha	The training rules of a monk or nun – 227 in the case of a Theravada monk.
Pitaka		*Basket.* Collection of scriptures (see Tipitaka).
Rupa	Rupa	*Form.* Used of an image of the Buddha; also, the first of the Five Khandhas.
Sakyamuni	Shakyamuni	*Sage of the Shakyas* (the tribe of the Buddha). Title of the historical Buddha.
Samadhi	Samadhi	*Meditative absorption.* A state of deep meditation.
Samatha	Samatha	A state of concentrated calmness; meditation (see Vipassana).
Samsara	Samsara	*Everyday life.* The continual round of birth, sickness, old age and death which can be transcended by following the Eightfold Path and Buddhist teaching.
Samudaya	Samudaya	*Arising; origin* (of suffering). The second Noble Truth.
Sangha	Sangha	*Community; assembly.* Often used for the order of bhikkhus and bhikkunis in Theravadin countries. In the Mahayana countries, the Sangha includes lay devotees and priests, eg in Japan.
Sankhara	Samskara	*Mental/karmic formation.* The fourth of the five Khandhas.
Sanna	Samjna	*Perception.* Third of the five Khandhas.
Satori (Japanese)		*Awakening.* A term used in Zen Buddhism.
Siddattha	Siddhartha	*Wish-fulfilled.* The personal name of the historical Buddha.
Sila	Sila	*Morality.*
Sutta	Sutra	*Text.* The word of the Buddha.
Sutta Pitaka	Sutra Pitaka	The second of the three collections – principally of teachings – that comprise the canon of basic scripture.
Tanha	Trishna	*Thirst; craving; desire* (rooted in ignorance). Desire as the cause of suffering. The second Noble Truth.

BUDDHISM

Buddhism

PALI	SANSKRIT	EXPLANATION
Tathagata	Tathagata	Another epithet for the Buddha.
Theravada	Sthaviravada	*Way of the elders.* A principal school of Buddhism, established in Sri Lanka and South East Asia. Also found in the West.
Thupa/Cetiya	Stupa	*Reliquary* (including pagodas).
Tipitaka	Tripitaka	*Three baskets.* A threefold collection of texts (Vinaya, Sutta, Abhidamma).
Tiratana	Triratna	*The triple refuge.* Buddha, the Dharmma and the Sangha. Another way of referring to the three jewels.
Tulku (Tibetan)		Reincarnated Lama.
Upaya		Any skilful means, eg meditation on loving kindness, to overcome anger.
Upekkha	Upeksa	*Equanimity; evenness of mind.*
	Vajrayana	*Thunderbolt; Diamond Way.* Teachings promulgated later, mainly in India and Tibet. Another term for esoteric Buddhism.
Vedana		*Feeling.* The second of the Five Khandhas.
Vihara		*Dwelling place; monastery.*
Vinaya		The rules of discipline of monastic life.
Vinaya Pitaka		The first of the three collections of the canon of basic scripture, containing mostly the discipline for monks and nuns, with many stories and some teachings.
Vinnana	Vijnana	*Consciousness.* The fifth of the Five Khandhas.
Vipassana	Vipashyana	Insight into the true nature of things. A particular form of meditation (see Samatha).
Viriya	Virya	*Energy; exertion.*
Wesak, or Vesak (Sinhalese)	Wesak	Buddha Day. Name of a festival and a month. On the full moon of Wesak (in May or June), the birth, Enlightenment and passing away of the Buddha took place, although some schools celebrate only the birth at this time, eg Zen.
Zazen (Japanese)		Meditation while seated, as in Zen Buddhism.
Zen (Japanese)		*Meditation.* Derived from the Sanskrit 'dhyana'. A school of Mahayana Buddhism that developed in China and Japan.

CHRISTIAN GLOSSARY

Unlike the other five world faiths included in this glossary, most of the terms given below are in English and will be familiar to many people. The historic languages of the Christian scriptures are Hebrew, Greek and Latin. The Old Testament was written largely in Hebrew, with some texts in Aramaic and Greek (Apocrypha). The whole of the Old Testament was translated into Greek, although many words and passages have their origin in Aramaic. Latin became increasingly the language of the Western Church from the 5th century AD when the Bible was translated into Latin.

PREFERRED FORM	MAIN VARIANTS	EXPLANATION
Absolution		The pronouncement by a priest of the forgiveness of sins.
AD	Anno Domini	*In the Year of our Lord.* The Christian calendar dates from the estimated date of the birth of Jesus Christ.
Advent		*Coming.* The period beginning on the fourth Sunday before Christmas (40 days before Christmas in the Eastern Orthodox tradition). A time of spiritual preparation for Christmas.
Agape		*The love of God.* New Testament word used for the common meal of Christians; a Love Feast.
Altar	Communion Table Holy Table	Table used for Eucharist, Mass, Lord's Supper. Some denominations refer to it as Holy Table or Communion Table.
Anglican		Churches in full communion with the See of Canterbury. Their origins and traditions are linked to the Church of England, and are part of the Anglican Communion.
Apocalyptic		(i) *Revelatory,* of God's present purposes and of the end of the world. (ii) Used of a literary genre, eg the Book of Revelation.
Apocrypha		Books of the Old Testament that are in the Greek but not the Hebrew Canon. Some Churches recognise the Apocrypha as part of the Old Testament Canon.
Apocryphal New Testament		A modern title for various early Christian books which are non-canonical.
Apostle		One who was sent out by Jesus Christ to preach the Gospel.
Ascension		The event, 40 days after the Resurrection, when Jesus 'ascended into heaven' (see Luke 24 and Acts 1).
Ash Wednesday		The first day of Lent. In some Churches, penitents receive the sign of the cross in ashes on their foreheads.

CHRISTIANITY

Christianity

PREFERRED FORM	MAIN VARIANTS	EXPLANATION
Atonement		Reconciliation between God and humanity; restoring a relationship broken by sin.
Baptism		Rite of initiation involving immersion in, or sprinkling or pouring of, water.
Baptist		(i) A member of the Baptist Church, which grew out of the Anabaptist movement during the 16th century Reformation. (ii) A Christian who practises Believer's Baptism.
Baptistry		(i) Building or pool used for baptism, particularly by immersion. (ii) Part of a church, where baptism takes place.
BC	Before Christ	Period of history before the estimated birth of Jesus Christ.
Believer's Baptism		The baptism of people who are old enough to understand the meaning of the rite.
Benediction		Blessing at the end of worship. Also, late afternoon or evening service including the blessing of the congregation with the consecrated host (usually in a Roman Catholic context).
Blessed Sacrament		Bread and wine which have been consecrated and set aside for future use (usually in the Roman Catholic Church).
Canon	Scripture	The accepted books of the Bible. The list varies between denominations.
Catholic		(i) *Universal*. (ii) Often used as an abbreviation for Roman Catholic.
Charismatic		A modern movement within the Church, emphasising spiritual gifts, such as healing or speaking with tongues.
Chrismation		(i) The Orthodox second sacrament of initiation by anointing with chrism (a special oil). Performed at the same time as baptism. (ii) Anointing with oil, eg healing or coronation.
Christ	Messiah	*The anointed one.* Messiah is used in the Jewish tradition to refer to the expected leader sent by God, who will bring salvation to God's people. Jesus' followers applied this title to him, and its Greek equivalent, Christ, is the source of the words Christian and Christianity.

10

Christianity

PREFERRED FORM	MAIN VARIANTS	EXPLANATION
Christmas		Festival commemorating the birth of Jesus Christ (25 December, in most Churches).
Church		(i) The whole community of Christians. (ii) The building in which Christians worship. (iii) A particular denomination.
Confession		Contrition; penance. (i) One of seven sacraments observed by some Churches whose priest confidentially hears a person's confession. (ii) An admission, by a Christian, of wrong-doing. (iii) A particular official statement (or profession) of faith.
Congregationalist		Member of a Christian body which believes that each local church is independent and self-governing under the authority of Christ.
Consubstantiation		Doctrine of the Eucharist associated with Luther, which holds that after consecration, the substances of the Body and Blood of Jesus Christ and of the bread and wine co-exist in union with each other.
Creed		Summary statement of religious beliefs, often recited in worship, especially the Apostles' and Nicene Creeds.
Crucifixion		Roman method of executing criminals and traitors by fastening them to a cross until they died of asphyxiation; used in the case of Jesus Christ and many who opposed the Romans.
Easter		Central Christian festival which celebrates the resurrection of Jesus Christ from the dead.
Ecumenism	Oikoumene	Movement within the Church towards co-operation and eventual unity.
Episcopacy		System of Church government by bishops.
Epistle	Letter	From the Greek word for letter. Several such letters or epistles, from Christian leaders to Christian Churches or individuals, are included in the New Testament.
Eucharist		*Thanksgiving.* A service celebrating the sacrificial death and resurrection of Jesus Christ, using elements of bread and wine (see Holy Communion).
Evangelical		Group, or church, placing particular emphasis on the Gospel and the scriptures as the sole authority in all matters of faith and conduct.
Evangelist		A writer of one of the four New Testament Gospels; a preacher of the gospel.

CHRISTIANITY

Christianity

PREFERRED FORM	MAIN VARIANTS	EXPLANATION
Font		Receptacle to hold water used in baptism.
Free Churches		Non-conformist denominations, free from state control (used of 20 Churches).
Good Friday		The Friday in Holy Week. Commemorates the day Jesus died on the cross.
Gospel	Evangel	(i) *Good news* (of salvation in Jesus Christ). (ii) An account of Jesus' life and work.
Grace		(i) The freely given and unmerited favour of God's love for humanity. (ii) Blessing. (iii) Prayer of thanks before or after meals.
Heaven		The place, or state, in which souls will be united with God after death.
Hell		The place, or state, in which souls will be separated from God after death.
Holy Communion		Central liturgical service observed by most Churches (see Eucharist, Mass, Lord's Supper, Liturgy). Recalls the last meal of Jesus, and celebrates his sacrificial and saving death.
Holy Spirit		The third person of the Holy Trinity. Active as divine presence and power in the world, and in dwelling in believers to make them like Christ and empower them to do God's will.
Holy Week		The week before Easter, when Christians recall the last week of Jesus' life on Earth.
Icon/Ikon		Painting or mosaic of Jesus Christ, the Virgin Mary, a saint, or a Church feast. Used as an aid to devotion, usually in the Orthodox tradition.
Iconostasis		Screen, covered with icons, used in Eastern Orthodox churches to separate the sanctuary from the nave.
Incarnation		The doctrine that God took human form in Jesus Christ. It is also the belief that God in Christ is active in the Church and in the world.
Jesus Christ		The central figure of Christian history and devotion. The second person of the Trinity.
Justification by Faith		The doctrine that God forgives ('treats as just') those who repent and believe in Jesus Christ.

Christianity

PREFERRED FORM	MAIN VARIANTS	EXPLANATION
Kerygma		The central message about Jesus proclaimed by the early Christians.
Kyrie (Greek)		*O Lord.* Addressed to Jesus, as in 'Kyrie eleison' (*Lord have mercy*).
Lectern		Stand supporting the Bible, often in the shape of an eagle.
Lectionary		List of scriptural passages for systematic reading throughout the year.
Lent		Penitential season. The 40 days leading up to Easter.
Liturgy		(i) Service of worship according to a prescribed ritual such as Evensong or Eucharist. (ii) Term used in the Orthodox Church for the Eucharist.
Logos		*Word.* Pre-existent Word of God incarnate as Jesus Christ.
Lord		Title used for Jesus to express his divine lordship over people, time and space.
Lord's Supper		Alternative term for Eucharist in some Churches (predominantly Non-conformist).
Lutheran		A major Protestant Church that receives its name from the 16th century German reformer, Martin Luther.
Mass		Term for the Eucharist, used by the Roman Catholic and other Churches.
Maundy Thursday		The Thursday in Holy Week. Commemorates the Last Supper.
Methodist		A Christian who belongs to the Methodist Church which came into existence through the work of John Wesley in the 18th century.
Missal		Book containing words and ceremonial directions for saying Mass.
Mother of God		The title given to the Virgin Mary, mainly in the Orthodox and Roman Catholic Churches, to underline the Trinitarian belief that Jesus was truly God (in this context, God refers to God incarnate as seen in Jesus Christ).

CHRISTIANITY

Christianity

PREFERRED FORM	MAIN VARIANTS	EXPLANATION
New Testament		Collection of 27 books forming the second section of the Canon of Christian Scriptures.
Non-conformist		Protestant Christian bodies which became separated from the established Church of England in the 17th century.
Old Testament		That part of the Canon of Christian Scriptures which the Church shares with Judaism, comprising 39 books covering the Hebrew Canon, and in the case of certain denominations, some books of the Apocrypha.
Ordination		In episcopal Churches, the 'laying on of hands' on priests and deacons by a bishop. In non-episcopal Churches, the 'laying on of hands' on ministers by other representatives of the Church.
Orthodox		(i) The Eastern Orthodox Church consisting of national Churches (mainly Greek or Slav), including the ancient Eastern Patriarchates. They hold the common Orthodox faith, and are in communion with the Patriarchate of Constantinople. (ii) Conforming to the creeds sanctioned by the ecumenical councils , eg Nicaea, Chalcedon.
Palm Sunday		The Sunday before Easter, commemorating the entry of Jesus into Jerusalem when he was acknowledged by crowds waving palm branches.
Paraclete	Comforter	*Advocate.* Term used for the Holy Spirit.
Parousia		*Presence.* The Second Coming or return of Jesus Christ.
Passion		The sufferings of Jesus Christ, especially in the time leading up to his crucifixion.
Patriarch		Title for principal Eastern Orthodox bishops. Also used for early Israelite leaders such as Abraham, Isaac, Jacob.
Pentecost	Whitsun	The Greek name for the Jewish Festival of Weeks, or Shavuot, which comes seven weeks ('fifty days') after Passover. On the day of this feast, the followers of Jesus received the gift of the Holy Spirit.
Pentecostalist		A Christian who belongs to a Church that emphasises certain gifts which were granted to the first believers on the Day of Pentecost (such as the power to heal the sick and speak in tongues).

Christianity

PREFERRED FORM	MAIN VARIANTS	EXPLANATION
Pope		The Bishop of Rome, head of the Roman Catholic Church.
Presbyterian		A member of a Church that is governed by elders or 'presbyters'; the national Church of Scotland.
Protestant		That part of the Church which became distinct from the Roman Catholic and Orthodox Churches when their members professed (or 'protested' – hence Protestant) the centrality of the Bible and other beliefs. Members affirm that the Bible, under the guidance of the Holy Spirit, is the ultimate authority for Christian teaching.
Pulpit		An elevated platform from which sermons are preached.
Purgatory		In some traditions, a condition or state in which good souls receive spiritual cleansing after death, in preparation for heaven.
Quaker		A member of the Religious Society of Friends, established through the work of George Fox in the 17th century.
Reconciliation	Confession	(i) Sacrament of the (Roman) Catholic Church, consisting of Contrition, Confession of sins, and Absolution. (ii) The human process of reconciling Christians with one another.
Redemption		Derived from the practice of paying the price of a slave's freedom; and so, the work of Jesus Christ in setting people free through his death.
Reformation		A 16th century reform movement that led to the formation of Protestant Churches. It emphasised the need to recover the initial beliefs and practices of the Church.
Resurrection		(i) The rising from the dead of Jesus Christ on the third day after the crucifixion. (ii) The rising from the dead of believers at the Last Day. (iii) The new, or risen, life of Christians.
Roman Catholic		That part of the Church owing loyalty to the Bishop of Rome, as distinct from Orthodox and Protestant Churches.
Sacrament		An outward sign of an inward blessing, as in baptism or the Eucharist.
Salvationist		A member of the Salvation Army founded by William and Catherine Booth in the 19th century.

Christianity

PREFERRED FORM	MAIN VARIANTS	EXPLANATION
Sanctification		The process by which a believer is made holy, to become like Jesus Christ.
Sin		(i) Act of rebellion or disobedience against the known will of God. (ii) An assessment of the human condition as disordered and in need of transformation.
Synoptic		*Having a common viewpoint.* It is applied to the presentation of Jesus' life in the first three gospels of Matthew, Mark and Luke in contrast with that given in the Gospel of John.
Tabernacle		(i) A receptacle for the Blessed Sacrament, not immediately consumed but set aside or 'reserved' (mainly in Roman Catholic and Eastern Orthodox Churches). The presence of the consecrated elements is usually signalled by a continuously burning light. (ii) Term used by some denominations of their building.
Transubstantiation		Roman Catholic doctrine concerning the Mass, defined at the Lateran Council of 1215, and confirmed at the Council of Trent in 1551. This states that in the Eucharist, at the words of consecration, the substance of the bread and wine becomes the substance of the Body and Blood of Jesus Christ, and that he is thus present on the altar.
Trinity		Three persons in one God; doctrine of the three-fold nature of God – Father, Son and Holy Spirit.
Unction	Sacrament of the Sick	The anointing with oil of a sick or dying person.
United Reformed Church		A Church formed by the union of English Congregationalists with the Presbyterian Church of England, and subsequently the Reformed Association of the Churches of Christ.
Vatican		The residence of the Pope in Rome, and the administrative centre of the Roman Catholic Church. The chief building of the Vatican is St Peter's Basilica, built on the traditional site of St Peter's tomb.
Virgin Birth		The doctrine of the miraculous conception of Jesus Christ by the Virgin Mary through the power of the Holy Spirit and without the agency of a human father.

HINDUISM GLOSSARY

The main references are to Sanskrit terminology, although variants are found and used in other Indian languages. Lakshmi, Laksmi, Vishnu or Vis Visnu type variants are not always included because of their frequency. Many of these terms will also be found in books on Buddhism and Sikhism, but with somewhat different meanings.

Proper names and place names are only included in this list if variant forms are commonly used.

PREFERRED FORM	MAIN VARIANTS	EXPLANATION
Acharya	Acarya	*One who teaches by example.* Usually refers to a prominent or exemplary spiritual teacher.
Advaita	Adwaita	*Non-dual.* Refers to the impersonalistic philosophy which unqualifyingly equates God, the soul and matter.
Ahimsa	Ahinsa	*Not killing.* Non-violence; respect for life.
Artha		Economic development. The second aim of life.
Arti	Arati	Welcoming ceremony in which auspicious articles such as incense and lamps are offered to the deity or to saintly people.
Aryan		*Noble.* Refers to those who know the spiritual values of life. Scholars say it refers to the original inhabitants of the Sindhu region in India.
Ashram	Asram	A place set up for spiritual development.
Ashrama	Asrama	A stage of life (of which there are four) adopted according to material considerations, but ultimately as a means to spiritual realisation.
Atharva Veda		The fourth of the *Vedas*.
Atman	Atma	*Self.* Can refer to body, mind or soul, depending on context. Ultimately, it refers to the real self, the soul.
Aum	Om	The sacred symbol and sound representing the ultimate; the most sacred of Hindu words.
Avatar	Avatara Avtara	*One who descends.* Refers to the descent of a deity, most commonly *Vishnu*. Sometimes it is translated as *incarnation* which, although inaccurate, may be the best English word available.
Ayodhya		Birthplace of *Rama*.

17

Hinduism

PREFERRED FORM	MAIN VARIANTS	EXPLANATION
Bhagavad Gita		*The Song of the Lord.* Spoken by Krishna, this is the most important scripture for most Hindus. Tradition dates it back to 3,000 years BCE, though most scholars attribute it to the first millennium BCE. Considered an Upanishad.
Bhajan	Bhajana	Devotional hymn or song.
Bhakti		*Devotion; love.* Devotional form of Hinduism.
Bhakti-yoga		The path of loving devotion, aimed at developing pure love of God.
Brahma		A Hindu deity, considered one of the Trimurti, and in charge of creative power; not to be confused with Brahman or Brahmin.
Brahmachari	Brahmacari Brahmacharin Brahmcarin	One in the first stage of life, a celibate student of Vedic knowledge.
Brahmacharya	Brahmacarya Brahma ch(c)ari Brahma ch(c)arin	The first ashrama or stage of life.
Brahman		The ultimate reality, or the all-pervading reality; that from which everything emanates, in which it rests and into which it is ultimately dissolved.
Brahmin	Brahman Brahmana	The first of the four varnas, the principal social groupings from which priests are drawn. Some writers, rather confusingly, use the spelling 'brahman', and the meaning only becomes clear in the context of a few sentences (see also Brahman and Brahma).
Darshan Shastras		Six systems of Hindu philosophy – Nyaya, Vaisheshika, Sankhya, Yoga, Vedanta and Meemansa.
Dassehra	Dussehra, Dassera, Dashara (Other variants are also found)	*Ten days.* Also called Vijay Dashami. Celebrates the victory of Rama on the tenth day of the bright half of the lunar month of Jyeshtha. As is often the case with Hindu festivals, followers may interpret the festival differently, eg in connection with Durga (see Navaratri).
Dharma		*Religion* or *religious duty* is the usual translation into English, but literally it means *the intrinsic quality of the self* or *that which sustains one's existence.*

18

Hinduism

PREFERRED FORM	MAIN VARIANTS	EXPLANATION
Dhoti		A garment made of natural fibre (usually cotton or silk), worn by males, which covers the lower body and legs.
Dhyana		Meditation.
Divali	Diwali, Dipavali, Deepavali	Festival of lights at the end of one year and beginning of the new year, according to one Hindu calendar.
Durga		Female deity. A form of the goddess Parvati; wife of Shiva.
Dvaita	Dwaita	*Dual.* Refers to the personalistic philosophy that differentiates between God, the soul and matter.
Dwarka	Dvarka Dvaraka Dwaraka	Pilgrimage site on the west coast of India.
Ganesha	Ganesh Ganupati Ganapati	A Hindu deity portrayed with an elephant's head – a sign of strength. The deity who removes obstacles.
Ganga		*The Ganges.* Most famous of all sacred rivers of India.
Gangotri		Source of the river Ganges.
Gotra		Exogamous group within Jati.
Grihastha	Gristhi Grhastha	The second stage of Hindu life; one who belongs to that stage, ie the householder (grihasti).
Guna		*Rope; quality.* Specifically refers to the three qualities of sattva (goodness), rajas (passion) and tamas (ignorance), which permeate and control matter.
Guru		Spiritual teacher, preceptor or enlightener.
Hanuman		The monkey warrior who faithfully served Rama and Sita. Also called Pavansuta (*son of the wind God*).
Havan		Also known as Agnihotra. The basis of many Hindu rituals used at weddings and on other ceremonial occasions; the ceremony or act of worship in which offerings of ghee and grains are made into fire.
Havan kund		The container, usually square or pyramid-shaped, in which the havan fire is burned.

HINDUISM

Hinduism

PREFERRED FORM	MAIN VARIANTS	EXPLANATION
Hitopadesh		Stories with a moral.
Holi		The festival of colours, celebrated in Spring.
Homa		Term often used interchangeably with havan.
The International Society for Krishna Consciousness (ISKCON)		A religious group of the Vaishnava tradition.
Janeu	Jenoi	Sacred thread worn by Hindus who study under a guru.
Janmashtami	Janmashtmi	The birthday of Krishna, celebrated on the eighth day of the waning moon in the month of Badra.
Japa	Jap	The quiet or silent repetition of a mantra as a meditative process.
Jati		*Caste* is the usual translation, meaning occupational kinship group.
Jnana	Gyan	*Knowledge.*
Jnana-yoga	Gyan-yoga	The path of knowledge, that aims at liberation.
Kali	Kaali	Name given to that power of God which delivers justice – often represented by the Goddess Kali (a form of Durga).
Kali yuga		The fourth of the ages; the iron age or the age of quarrelling and hypocrisy.
Kama		The third of the four aims of life – regulated sense of enjoyment.
Karma		*Action.* Used of work to refer to the law of cause and effect.
Karma-yoga		The path of self-realisation through dedicating the fruits of one's work to God.
Kirtan		Songs of praise; corporate devotional singing, usually accompanied by musical instruments.
Krishna		Usually considered an avatar of Vishnu. One of the most popular of all Hindu deities in contemporary Britain. His teachings are found in the Bhagavad Gita.
Kshatriya	Khatri	Second of the four varnas of traditional Hindu society, the ruling or warrior class.

Hinduism

PREFERRED FORM	MAIN VARIANTS	EXPLANATION
Lakshmi	Laksmi	The goddess of fortune.
Mahabharata		The Hindu epic that relates the story of the five Pandava princes. It includes the Bhagavad Gita.
Mala	Maala	Circle of stringed beads of wood or wool used in meditation.
Mandala	Mandal	A circle, area or community/group.
Mandir		*Temple.*
Mantra		That which delivers the mind. Refers to a short sacred text or prayer, often recited repetitiously.
Manusmriti		The laws of Manu. An ancient and important text on Dharma, including personal and social laws.
Marg		*Path* (see Jnana yoga, Karma yoga and Bhakti yoga).
Mata		*Mother.* Often associated with Hindu goddesses who represent shakti (power).
Mathura		Holy place connected with Krishna.
Maya		*Not this.* Usually, it refers to illusion, particularly where the permanent soul identifies itself with temporary matter, eg the body, etc. It can also mean *power*.
Moksha	Moksa	Ultimate liberation from the process of transmigration, the continuous cycle of birth and death.
Mundan		The head-shaving ceremony. Performed in the first or third year of life.
Murti	Moorti	*Form.* The image or deity used as a focus of worship. 'Idol' should definitely not be used, and 'statue' may also cause offence.
Navaratri	Navaratra	The Nine Nights Festival preceding Dassehra, and held in honour of the goddess Durga.
Nirvana		The cessation of material existence.
Panchatantra		Part of the supplementary Vedic scriptures, composed of animal stories with a moral.
Parvati		The consort of Shiva, also known by other names such as Durga, Devi, etc.

Hinduism

PREFERRED FORM	MAIN VARIANTS	EXPLANATION
Prahlada	Prahalada	A great devotee of Vishnu, connected with the festival of Holi.
Pranayam	Pranayama	Regulation of breath as a means of controlling the mind.
Prashad	Prasad Prasada Prashada	Sacred or sanctified food.
Pravachan		A lecture or talk, usually based on the scriptures.
Puja	Pooja	*Worship.* General term referring to a variety of practices in the home or Mandir.
Purana		*Ancient.* Part of the Smriti scriptures. Contains many of the well-known stories of Hinduism.
Raja Yoga	Raj Yoga	Path of self-control and meditation to realise God.
Rajas		Passion or creative potency, one of the three gunas (qualities of material nature).
Rakhi	Raakhi	A bracelet, usually made out of silk or cotton, tied to give protection and to strengthen the bond of mutual love.
Raksha Bandhan		The festival when women tie a decorative bracelet on their brothers' wrists.
Rama		The incarnation of the Lord, and hero of the Ramayana (avoid using the variant 'Ram' for obvious reasons).
Ramayana	Ramayan	The Hindu epic that relates the story of Rama and Sita, composed by the sage Valmiki thousands of years ago.
Ramnavami	Ramnavmi	The birthday festival of Rama.
Rig Veda	Rg or Rc Veda	The first scripture of Hinduism, containing spiritual and scientific knowledge.
Rishi	Rsi, risi	A spiritually wise person. More specifically, one of the seven seers who received the divine wisdom.
Sadhana	Sadhan	One's regulated spiritual practices or discipline.
Sadhu	Saddhu	Holy man, ascetic.
Sama Veda		The Veda of chanting; material mainly from the Rig Veda, arranged for ritual chanting in worship.

Hinduism

PREFERRED FORM	MAIN VARIANTS	EXPLANATION
Samsara	Sansara	The world – the place where transmigration (the soul's passage through a series of lives in different species) occurs.
Samskar	Sanskar, Samskara	Sacraments designed to initiate a new stage of life. There is usually a total of sixteen such rites of passage (though many schools of thought do not practise them all).
Sanatan Dharma		The eternal or imperishable religion; also known as Vedic Dharma. Adherents often prefer this term to Hinduism since it characterises their belief in the revealed and universal nature of religion.
Sannyasa		The state of renunciation, the fourth stage of life.
Sannyasin	Samyasin, Samnyasin	A renunciate who, having given up worldly affairs and attachments, has entered the fourth stage of life, often as a mendicant.
Sanskrit		Sacred language of the Hindu scriptures.
Saraswati		The power of knowledge, often represented by the goddess Saraswati, the goddess of learning.
Sattva	Sattwa	*Goodness,* or the potency to sustain and nourish; one of the three gunas.
Seva	Sewa	Service, either to the divine or to humanity.
Shaivism	Saivism	The religion of Hindus who are devotees of Shiva.
Shakti	Sakti	Energy or power, especially of a Hindu feminine deity.
Shiva	Siva (many variants – even Civa – have been found)	A Hindu god. The name means *kindly* or *auspicious.*
Shivaratri	Sivaratri	The annual festival celebrated in February/March in honour of Shiva. Also called Mahashivaratri.
Shraddha	Sraddha	Ceremony in which sanctified food is offered to the poor and needy in memory of departed ancestors.
Shri	Sri	*Illustrious.* Used as a title of respect, eg Shri Krishna. Also a respectful title for men. The feminine form is Shrimati (Mrs).
Shruti	Srti	*That which is remembered.* Applicable to Hindu scriptures other than the Vedas.
Sita	Seeta	The divine consort of Rama.

Hinduism

PREFERRED FORM	MAIN VARIANTS	EXPLANATION
Smriti	Srti, Shruti	*That which is heard.* A term specifically applied to the four Vedas, including the Upanishads. Some Hindus believe that Smriti is subservient to Shruti, but other Hindus consider them to have equal importance.
Sutra	Sutta	Short sayings or verses relating to various rituals, or encapsulating profound philosophical meaning.
Swami	Svami	*Controller.* Sometimes, more specifically, Goswami *(one who can control his/her senses).* An honorific title applied to a religious teacher or holy person, particularly the sannyasi.
Swastika	Svastika	From the Sanskrit for well-being; a mark of good fortune. The four arms signify the four directions (space), the four Vedas (knowledge), and the four stages (time) in the life cycle. Not to be confused with the Nazi symbol.
Tamas		Ignorance or destructive potency; the lowest of the three gunas.
Trimurti		*The three deities.* Refers to Brahma, Vishnu and Shiva, who personify and control the three gunas. They represent and control the three functions of creation, preservation and destruction. 'Trinity' should be avoided.
Upanayana		Ceremony when the sacred thread is tied – to mark the start of learning with a guru.
Upanishad	Upanisad	*To sit down near.* A sacred text based on the teaching of a guru to a disciple. The Upanishads explain the teachings of the Vedas.
Vaishnavism	Vaisnavism	The religion of Hindus who are devotees of the god Vishnu.
Vaishya	Vaisya	The third of the four varnas of Hindu society, composed of merchants and farmers.
Vanaprastha		The third stage of life, typified by retirement and asceticism.
Vanaprasthi	Vanaprastha	*Forest dweller.* One who is in the third stage of life.
Varanasi	Banares, Benares, Kashi, Kasi	City on the river Ganges, sacred to Shiva. It is one of the holiest pilgrimage sites and also an ancient centre of learning.

Hinduism

PREFERRED FORM	MAIN VARIANTS	EXPLANATION
Varna		*Colour.* The four principal divisions of Hindu society. It is important to note that the word 'caste' refers strictly to sub-divisions within each varna, and not to varnas themselves.
Varnashrama	Varnasrama Dharma	The system whereby society is divided into four varnas (divisions), and life into four ashramas (stages).
Varsha Pratipada		The day of Creation, celebrated as New Year's Day by many Hindus.
Veda		*Knowledge.* Specifically refers to the four Vedas, though any teaching which is consistent with the conclusions of these scriptures is also accepted as Vedic.
Vijay Dashmi	Vijaya Dashami	Another name for Dassehra.
Vishnu	Visnu	A Hindu god. With Brahma and Shiva forms the Trimurti.
Vrat	Vratam	*Vow.* Often including abstention from certain foods.
Vrindavan	Brindavan Vrindavana Brindaban	The sacred village connected with Krishna's pastimes as a youth.
Yajur Veda		One of the four Vedas, dealing with the knowledge of karma.
Yamuna	Jamuna, Jumna	Tributary of the river Ganga (*Ganges*), considered by many Hindus to be the most sacred of all holy rivers.
Yatra	Jatra	*Pilgrimage.* Usually to important sacred places in India.
Yoga		Communion; union of the soul with the Supreme, or a process which promotes that relationship. The English word 'yoke' is derived from yoga.
Yuga		*Age,* or extended period of time, of which there are four.

ISLAM GLOSSARY

ﷺ – This Arabic 'logo-type' is composed of the words 'Salla-llahu alaihi wa sallam' – peace and blessings of Allah upon him. They are used by Muslims every time the Prophet Muhammad ﷺ is mentioned. Similar respect is accorded to the other Prophets.

The Qur'an was revealed in Arabic, therefore Arabic is the language of Islam, Islamic worship, theology, ethics and jurisprudence. Islam is inextricably linked with the Arabic language despite the variety of languages spoken by the believers.

For British teachers and pupils who have not encountered Islamic terms, this transliteration is a simplified version of that used by contemporary scholars. An apostrophe is used to indicate a pause. The reader will note that the words salah and zakah end in 'h' when they appear alone. When part of a phrase, these words are written with a 't' at the end, eg Salat-ul-Zuhr, Zakat-ul-Fitr, as a guide to pronunciation.

TERM	EXPLANATION
Abd	*Servant.* As in Abdullah, servant of Allah.
Abu Bakr	The first Khalifah, successor to the leadership of the Muslim community after the death of the Prophet Muhammad ﷺ.
Adam	Adam (peace be upon him). The first man, and first Prophet of Allah.
Adhan	Call to prayer. From the same root, Mu'adhin (one who makes the call to prayer).
Aishah	One of the wives of the Prophet Muhammad ﷺ, and daughter of Abu Bakr (Radhi-Allahu-anhum – *may Allah be pleased with them*).
Akhirah	Everlasting life after death – the hereafter.
Akhlaq	Conduct, character, attitudes and ethics.
al-Amin	*The Trustworthy.* The name by which Prophet Muhammad ﷺ was generally known, even before the revelation of Islam.
al-Aqsa	Masjid-ul-Aqsa (*The Farthest Mosque*) in Jerusalem, often known as the Dome of the Rock.
al-Fatihah	*The Opener.* Surah 1 of the Qur'an. Recited at least 17 times daily during the five times of salah. Also known as 'The Essence' of the Qur'an.
al-hamdu-li-Llah	*All praise belongs to Allah.* Frequently used as an expression of thanks to Allah.
al-Kafi	The title of the books of Hadith compiled by Muhammad ibn-Yaqub Koleini, a Shi'ah scholar.
al-Khulafa-ur-Rashidun	*The Rightly Guided Khalifahs.* The first four successors to the leadership role of the Prophet Muhammad ﷺ. They were Abu Bakr, Umar, Uthman and Ali (Radhi-Allahu-anhum – *may Allah be pleased with them*).
al-Madinah	Madinatu'n-Nabi (*The City of the Prophet*). The name given to Yathrib after the Prophet Muhammad ﷺ migrated there in 622 CE and founded the first Islamic state.

Islam

TERM	EXPLANATION
Ali	Cousin and son-in-law of the Prophet Muhammad ﷺ; husband of Fatimah Zahrah; father of Hassan, Hussein, and Zainab; the fourth of 'al-Khulafa ur-Rashidun' according to Sunnis, and the first successor accepted by Shi'ah Islam (Radhi-Allahu-anhum – *may Allah be pleased with them*).
Allah	The Islamic name for God in the Arabic language. Used in preference to the word God, this Arabic term is singular, has no plural, nor is it associated with masculine, feminine or neuter characteristics.
Allahu Akbar	*Allah is most great.*
Angels	Beings created by Allah from light. They have no free will and are completely obedient to Allah.
Ansar	*Supporters.* The Muslims of al-Madinah, who welcomed, helped and supported the Muslims who migrated from Makkah.
Arafat	A plain, a few kilometres from Makkah, where pilgrims gather to worship, pray and ask for forgiveness. This takes place on the ninth day of the Islamic month of Dhul-Hijjah, the day before Id-ul-Adha.
Asr (Salat-ul-Asr)	Mid-afternoon salah which may be performed from late afternoon until a short while before sunset.
As-Salamu-Alaykum	*Peace be upon you.* An Islamic greeting.
Ayah (sing.)	A unit within a Surah of the Qur'an.
Barakah	Blessings.
Bilal	The first Mu'adhin of Islam (see Adhan), a companion of Prophet Muhammad ﷺ, formerly an Abyssinian slave (Radhi-Allahu-anhu – *may Allah be pleased with him*).
Bismillah	*In the name of Allah.*
Bismillah-ir-Rahman-ir-Rahim	*In the name of Allah – All Gracious, All Merciful.* The preface to all Surahs of the Qur'an except the ninth one. It is usually said by Muslims before eating or beginning any action.
Dar-ul-Islam	*House* or *abode of Islam.* Sometimes used to refer to lands ruled by Islamic Shari'ah.
Da'wah	*Call.* Inviting people to Islam, whether by literal invitation and preaching, or by the example of good actions.
Dawud	David (peace be upon him). A Prophet of Allah to whom the Zabur (the Book of Psalms) was given.
Dhikr	*Remembrance.* Remembrance of Allah in one's heart or by reciting His names or sections from the Qur'an.
Dhimmi	A non-Muslim living freely under the protection of an Islamic state.

27

Islam

TERM	EXPLANATION
Dhul-Hijjah	The month of the Hajj, last month of the Islamic year.
Din	Way of life, religion together with its practices.
Din-ul-Fitrah	A description of Islam as the natural way of life.
Du'a	Varying forms of personal prayer and supplication.
Fajr (Salat-ul-Fajr)	Dawn salah which may be performed from dawn until just before sunrise.
Fard	Obligatory duty according to divine law, eg offering salah five times a day.
Fatihah	See al-Fatihah.
Fatimah (al-Zahrah)	Daughter of the Prophet Muhammad ﷺ; wife of Ali; mother of Hassan, Hussein and Zainab (Radhi-Allahu-anhum – *may Allah be pleased with them*).
Fatwa	The legal guidance of a pious, just, knowledgeable Muslim scholar and jurist, based on the Qur'an, Sunnah and Islamic Shari'ah.
Fiqh	*Understanding.* Islamic jurisprudence.
Ghusl	Greater ablution. Formal washing of the whole body prior to worship (see Wudu).
Hadith	Saying; report; account. The sayings of the Prophet Muhammad ﷺ, as recounted by his household, progeny and companions. These are a major source of Islamic law. Some Hadith are referred to as Hadith Qudsi (*sacred Hadith*) having been divinely communicated to the Prophet Muhammad ﷺ.
Hafiz	Someone who knows the whole Qur'an by heart.
Hajar	Hagar. Wife of the Prophet Ibrahim, and mother of the Prophet Isma'il (peace be upon them).
Hajj	Annual pilgrimage to Makkah, which each Muslim must undertake at least once in a lifetime if he or she has the health and wealth. A Muslim male who has completed Hajj is called Hajji, and a female, Hajjah.
Halal	Any action or thing which is permitted or lawful.
Haram	Anything unlawful or not permitted.
Haram Sharif	The grand mosque in Makkah, which encompasses the Ka'bah, the hills of Safa and Marwah and the well of Zamzam.
Hijab	*Veil.* Often used to describe the head scarf or modest dress worn by women, who are required to cover everything except face and hands in the sight of anyone other than immediate family.
Hijrah	*Departure; exit; emigration.* The emigration of the Prophet Muhammad ﷺ from Makkah to Madinah in 622 CE. The Islamic calendar commences from this event.

ISLAM

28

Islam

TERM	EXPLANATION
Hira	The name of a place near Makkah, where the Prophet Muhammad ﷺ went for solitude and worship. It was there that he received the first revelation of the Qur'an.
Ibadah	All acts of worship. Any permissible action performed with the intention to obey Allah.
Iblis	The Jinn who defied Allah by refusing to bow to Adam (peace be upon him), and later became the tempter of all human beings (see Shaytan).
Ibrahim	*Abraham* (peace be upon him). A Prophet of Allah to whom the 'scrolls' were given.
Id	*Recurring happiness.* A religious holiday; a feast for thanking Allah and celebrating a happy occasion.
Id Mubarak	Id blessings! Greeting exchanged during Islamic celebrations.
Id-ul-Adha	Celebration of the sacrifice, commemorating the Prophet Ibrahim's willingness to sacrifice his son Isma'il for Allah (peace be upon them). Also known as Id-ul-Kabir – *the Greater Id* – and Qurban Bayram (Turkish) – *feast of sacrifice.*
Id-ul-Fitr	Celebration of breaking the fast on the day after Ramadan ends, which is also the first day of Shawal, the tenth Islamic month. Also known as Id-ul-Saghir – *the Lesser Id* – and Sheker Bayram (Turkish) – *sugar feast.*
Ihram	The state or condition entered into to perform either Hajj or Umrah. During this period, many normally permitted actions are placed out of bounds to Muslims. Also, the name of the two plain white unsewn cloths worn by male pilgrims to indicate the brotherhood, equality and purity of the pilgrim. For women, the dress of Ihram consists of their normal modest clothing.
Ijma	General consensus of scholars, expressed or tacit, on matters of law and practice.
Imam	*Leader.* A person who leads the communal prayer, or a founder of an Islamic school of jurisprudence. In Shi'ah Islam, Imam is also the title of Ali (Radhi-Allahu-anhu – *may Allah be pleased with him*) and his successors.
Imamah	Office and function of an Imam. Religious authority in Shi'ah Islam; successor to the Prophet Muhammad ﷺ as leader of the Muslim community.
Iman	Faith.
Injil	*Gospel.* A book given to Prophet Isa (peace be upon him).
Iqamah	Call to stand up for salah.
Isa	Jesus. A Prophet of Allah, born of the virgin Mary (peace be upon them).
Isha (Salat-ul-Isha)	Evening salah which may be performed from just over an hour after sunset, until midnight.
Islam	Peace attained through willing obedience to Allah's divine guidance.

Islam

TERM	EXPLANATION
Isma'il	*Ishmael.* A Prophet of Allah. Son of the Prophet Ibrahim and Hajar (peace be upon them).
Isnad	Chain of transmission of each Hadith.
Jibril	*Gabriel.* The angel who delivered Allah's messages to His Prophets.
Jihad	Personal individual struggle against evil in the way of Allah. It can also be collective defence of the Muslim community.
Jinn	Being created by Allah from fire.
Jumu'ah (Salat-ul-Jumu'ah)	The weekly communal salah, and attendance at the khutbah performed shortly after midday on Fridays.
Ka'bah	A cube-shaped structure in the centre of the grand mosque in Makkah. The first house built for the worship of the One True God.
Khadijah	First wife of the Prophet Muhammad ﷺ. Mother of Fatimah Zahrah (*Radhi-Allahu-anhum – may Allah be pleased with them*).
Khalifah	Successor; inheritor; custodian; vice-regent (see al-Khulafa-ur-Rashidun).
Khilafah	The institution of the Khalifah
Khums	Contribution (additional to zakah) of one fifth of surplus annual income paid by Shi'ah Muslims. Sunni Muslims only apply Khums to booty.
Khutbah	*Speech.* Talk delivered on special occasions such as the Jum'uah and Id prayers.
Laylat-ul-Qadr	The Night of Power, when the first revelation of the Qur'an was made to Prophet Muhammad ﷺ. It is believed to be one of the last ten nights of Ramadan.
Madinah	See al-Madinah.
Maghrib (Salat-ul-Maghrib)	Sunset salah which is performed after sunset until daylight ends.
Mahdi, al-Muntazar	The (rightly) guided one who is awaited and will appear towards the end of time to lead the Ummah and restore justice on Earth. The one who is promised in the Judaic, Christian and Islamic traditions.
Makkah	City where the Prophet Muhammad ﷺ was born, and where the Ka'bah is located.
Maryam	Mary. The virgin mother of the Prophet Isa (peace be upon them).
Masjid	*Place of prostration.* Mosque.

Islam

TERM	EXPLANATION
Mihrab	Niche or alcove in a mosque wall, indicating the Qiblah – the direction of Makkah, towards which all Muslims face to perform salah.
Mina	Place near Makkah, where pilgrims stay on the 10th, 11th and 12th of Dhul-Hijjah and perform some of the activities of the Hajj.
Minbar	Rostrum; platform; dais. The stand from which the Imam delivers the khutbah or speech in the mosque or praying ground.
Miqat	*Place appointed,* at which pilgrims enter into the state of ihram.
Mi'raj	The ascent through the heavens of the Prophet Muhammad ﷺ.
Mu'adhin	Caller to prayer (see Adhan). Known in English as 'muezzin'.
Muhammad ﷺ	*Praised.* Name of the final Prophet ﷺ.
Muharram	First month in the Islamic calendar, which is calculated from the time the Prophet Muhammad ﷺ migrated to Yathrib (Madinah).
Musa	Moses (peace be upon him). A Prophet of Allah to whom the Tawrah (Torah) was given.
Mumin	Faithful. A believer, a practicing Muslim who wholeheartedly yields to Allah's guiding wisdom and is thus in harmony with His will and at peace with himself and fellow creatures.
Muslim	One who claims to have accepted Islam by professing the Shahadah.
Muzdalifah	Place where pilgrims on Hajj stop for a time during the night of the day they spend at Arafat.
Nabi	Prophet of Allah.
Niyyah	Intention. A legally required statement of intent, made prior to all acts of devotion such as salah, Hajj or sawm.
Qadar	Allah's complete and final control over the fulfilment of events or destiny.
Qiblah	Direction which Muslims face when performing salah – towards the Ka'bah (see Mihrab).
Qur'an	That which is read or recited. The Divine Book revealed to the Prophet Muhammad ﷺ. Allah's final revelation to humankind.
Rak'ah	A unit of salah, made up of recitation, standing, bowing and two prostrations.
Ramadan	The ninth month of the Islamic calendar, during which fasting is required from just before dawn until sunset, as ordered by Allah in the Qur'an.
Rasul	Messenger of Allah.

Islam

TERM	EXPLANATION
Sa'y	Walking and hastening between Safa and Marwah, as part of the Hajj, in remembrance of Hajar's search for water for her son Isma'il (peace be upon them).
Sadaqah	Voluntary payment or good action for charitable purposes.
Safa & Marwah	Two hills in Makkah, near the Ka'bah, now included within the grand mosque (see Sa'y).
Sahih al-Bukhari	The title of the books of Hadith compiled by Muhammad ibn Isma'il al-Bukhari, a Sunni scholar. The collection is described as Sahih (authentic).
Sahih Muslim	The title of the books of Hadith compiled by Abul Husayn Muslim ibn al-Hajjaj, a Sunni scholar. The collection is described as Sahih (authentic).
Salah	Prescribed communication with, and worship of, Allah, performed under specific conditions, in the manner taught by the Prophet Muhammad ﷺ, and recited in the Arabic language. The five daily times of salah are fixed by Allah.
Sawm	Fasting from just before dawn until sunset. Abstinence is required from all food and drink (including water) as well as smoking and conjugal relations.
Shahadah	Declaration of faith, which consists of the statement, 'There is no god except Allah, Muhammad is the Messenger of Allah'.
Shari'ah	Islamic law based upon the Qur'an and Sunnah.
Shaytan	*Rebellious; proud.* The devil (see Iblis).
Shi'ah	*Followers.* Muslims who believe in the Imamah, successorship of Ali (Radhi-Allahu-anhu – *may Allah be pleased with him*) after the Prophet Muhammad ﷺ and 11 of his most pious, knowledgeable descendants.
Shirk	*Association.* Regarding anything as being equal or partner to Allah. Shirk is forbidden in Islam.
Shura	Consultation of the people in the management of religious and worldly affairs. A duty prescribed in the Qur'an to leaders at all levels, from family to government.
Sirah	Biographical writings about the conduct and example of the Prophet Muhammad ﷺ.
Subhah	String of beads used to count recitations in worship.
Sunnah	Model practices, customs and traditions of the Prophet Muhammad ﷺ. This is found in both Hadith and Sirah.
Sunni	Muslims who believe in the successorship of Abu Bakr, Umar, Uthman and Ali (Radhi-Allahu-anhum – *may Allah be pleased with them*) after the Prophet Muhammad ﷺ.
Surah	Division of the Qur'an (114 in all).

Islam

TERM	EXPLANATION
Takbir	Saying 'Allahu Akbar!' Recited during salah, Id and other celebratory occasions.
Tawaf	Walking seven times around the Ka'bah in worship of Allah. Also, a part of Hajj and Umrah.
Tawhid	Belief in the Oneness of Allah – absolute monotheism as practiced in Islam.
Tawrah	*The Torah.* The book given to the Prophet Musa (Moses) (peace be upon him).
Ulama	Scholars of Islamic law and jurisprudence (sing. Alim).
Umar ibn ul-Khattab	Second Khalifah of Islam.
Ummah	Community. World-wide community of Muslims; the nation of Islam.
Umrah	Lesser pilgrimage which can be performed at any time of the year.
Uthman	The third Khalifah of Islam.
Wudu	Ablution before salah.
Yathrib	Town to which the Prophet Muhammad migrated from Makkah (see al-Madinah).
Zabur	The Book of Psalms given to Prophet Dawud (David) (peace be upon him).
Zakah	Purification of wealth by payment of annual welfare due. An obligatory act of worship.
Zakat-ul-Fitr	Welfare payment at the end of Ramadan.
Zamzam	Name of the well adjacent to the Ka'bah in Makkah. The water first sprang in answer to Hajar's search and prayers (see Hajar and Sa'y).
Zuhr (Salat-ul-Zuhr)	Salah which can be performed after midday until afternoon.

JUDAISM GLOSSARY

Most of the terms included in this section are Hebrew in origin. However, since the Jewish diaspora, many terms reflect the different countries where Jews have settled. For example, many words are in Yiddish, a common language (a mixture of German, Russian and Hebrew) developed by Jews throughout Central and Eastern Europe. The preferred form in this glossary uses the Sephardic pronunciation, which is equivalent to modern Hebrew as spoken in Israel today. As with all transliterations, there may be acceptable differences in the ways in which words are spelt.

PREFERRED FORM	MAIN VARIANTS	EXPLANATION
Afikomen (Greek)		*Dessert.* Portion of a matzah eaten near the end of the Seder.
Agadah	Aggadah	*Telling.* Rabbinical teachings on moral values.
Aleinu		Key prayer at the conclusion of each service.
Aliyah		*To go up.* (i) Being called to read the Sefer Torah in the synagogue. (ii) The migration of Jews to Israel.
Amidah		*Standing.* The standing prayer.
Aron Hakodesh		*Holy Ark.* The focal point of the synagogue, containing Torah scrolls.
Ashkenazim		Jews of Central and Eastern European origin.
Bar Mitzvah		*Son of Commandment.* A boy's coming of age at 13 years old, usually marked by a synagogue ceremony and family celebration.
Bat Mitzvah	Bat Chayil	*Daughter of Commandment.* As above, but for girls from 12 years old. May be marked differently between communities.
Bet ha Knesset	Beit ha Knesset Shul	*House of Assembly.* Synagogue.
Bimah		*Dais.* Raised platform primarily for reading the Torah in the synagogue.
Brit Milah	Berit Milah, Bris	*Circumcision.*
Challah	Hallah	Enriched bread used particularly on Shabbat and during festivals.
Chazan	Hazzan Cantor	Leader of reading, singing and chanting in the services of some synagogues.
Chumash		*Five.* The Torah in book form, used in the synagogue and the home.

34

Judaism

PREFERRED FORM	MAIN VARIANTS	EXPLANATION
Circumcision		Religious rite of Brit Milah, perfomed by a qualified mohel on all Jewish boys, usually on the eighth day after birth.
Gemara	Gemarah	Commentary on the Mishnah included in the Talmud.
Genizah		Storage place for damaged religious texts.
Haftarah		*Completion.* Passages from Nevi'im (Prophets) read in the synagogue (linked to weekly Torah and festival readings).
Hagadah	Haggadah	*Telling.* A book used at Seder.
Halakhah	Halacha	*The Way.* The code of conduct encompassing all aspects of Jewish life.
Hanukiah	Chanukiah Menorah	Nine-branched Hanukkah lamp used at the festival of Hanukkah.
Hanukkah	Chanukah	*Dedication.* An eight-day festival of lights to celebrate the re-dedication of the temple following the Maccabean victory over the Greeks.
Hasid	Chasid Hasidim (pl.) Chasidim	*Pious.* Member of the Orthodox movement of Hasidism.
Hasidism	Chasidism	A religious and social movement formed by Israel Baal Shem Tov (from the 18th century onwards).
Havdalah		*Distinction.* Ceremony marking the conclusion of Shabbat.
Hebrew	Ivrit	Ancient Semitic language; language of the Tenakh (Hebrew Scriptures) and used by Jews for prayer and study. Also, everyday language in Israel.
Huppah	Chuppah	Canopy used for a wedding ceremony, under which the bride and groom stand.
Israel		*One who struggles with God.* The phrase refers to the world-wide Jewish community; the land of Israel and the modern state of Israel.
Kabbalah	Cabala	Jewish mysticism.
Kaddish		Prayer publicly recited by mourners.
Kashrut		Laws relating to keeping a kosher home and lifestyle.

Judaism

PREFERRED FORM	MAIN VARIANTS	EXPLANATION
Ketubah	Ketubbah	Document that defines rights and obligations within Jewish marriage.
Ketuvim		*Writings.* Third section of the Tenakh.
Kibbutz	Kibbutzim (pl.)	Israeli collective village based on socialist principles.
Kiddush		*Holy.* A prayer sanctifying Shabbat and festival days, usually recited over wine.
Kippah	Yamulkah Capel	Head covering worn during prayers, Torah study, etc. Some followers wear it constantly.
Knesset		*Assembly.* Israeli parliament.
Kol Nidrei	Kol Nidre	*All vows.* Prayer recited on the evening of Yom Kippur.
Korach		Name of the leader who defied Moses in the wilderness
Kosher	Kasher	*Fit; proper.* Foods permitted by Jewish dietary laws.
Ladino		Language used predominately by Sephardim.
Magen David		*Shield of David*, popularly called Star of David.
Maimonides		*Rabbi Moses ben Maimon* (1135-1204), a leading Jewish philosopher, medical writer and codifier of Jewish law.
Mashiach	Moshiach Messiah	*The annointed one* who will herald in a new era for Judaism and all humankind.
Matzah	Matzot (pl.)	A flat cracker-like bread which has been baked before it rises; used at Pesach.
Menorah		Seven-branched candelabrum which was lit daily in the Temple.
Mezuzah		A scroll placed on doorposts of Jewish homes, containing a section from the Torah and often enclosed in a decorative case.
Midrash		Collections of various Rabbinic commentaries on the Tenakh.
Mikveh		Ritual bath used for the immersion of people and objects.

Judaism

PREFERRED FORM	MAIN VARIANTS	EXPLANATION
Minyan		Quorum of ten men, over Bar Mitzvah age, required for a service. Progressive communities may include women but do not always require a minyan.
Mishnah		First writing down of the Oral Tradition. An authoritative document forming part of the Talmud, codified about 200 CE.
Mishkan		*Dwelling.* The original travelling sanctuary used prior to the building of the permanent Temple in Jerusalem.
Mitzvah	Mitzvot (pl.)	*Commandment.* The Torah contains 613 Mitzvot. Commonly used to describe good deeds.
Mohel		Person trained to perform Brit Milah.
Moshav	Moshavim (pl.)	Collective village or farm in Israel.
Ner Tamid		*Eternal light.* The perpetual light above the Aron Hakodesh.
Nevi'im		*Prophets.* Second section of the Tenakh.
Noachide Laws		Seven laws given to Noah after the flood, which are incumbent on all humankind. These laws form the foundation for a just society.
Parev	Parveh	Neutral foods, which are neither milk nor meat, eg vegetables, eggs, fish.
Pesach	Passover	Festival commemorating the Exodus from Egypt. One of the three biblical pilgrim festivals. Pesach is celebrated in the spring.
Pikei Avot	Pirke Avoth	*Sayings of the Fathers.* Part of the Mishnah containing ethics of Rabbinical sages.
Pikuakh Nefesh		*Save a soul.* The setting aside of certain laws in order to save a life.
Progrom		Organised attack on Jews, especially frequent in 19th and early 20th century Eastern Europe.
Purim		Festival commemorating the rescue of Persian Jewry as told in the book of Esther.
Rabbi		*My teacher.* An ordained Jewish teacher. Often the religious leader of a Jewish community.

Judaism

PREFERRED FORM	MAIN VARIANTS	EXPLANATION
Rashi		*Rabbi Shlomo ben Yitzhak (1040 – 1105).* A French rabbinical scholar and leading commentator on the Torah and Talmud.
Rebbe		*Rabbi.* The term used by Hasidim for their religious leader.
Rosh Hashanah	Rosh Ha-Shanah	*Head of the Year.* Jewish New Year.
Seder		*Order.* A home-based ceremonial meal during Pesach, at which the Exodus from Egypt is recounted using the Hagadah.
Sefer Torah		Torah scroll. The five books of Moses handwritten on parchment and rolled to form a scroll.
Sephardim	Sefardim	Jews originating from Mediterranean countries, especially Spain, North Africa and the Middle East.
Shabbat	Shabbos	Day of spiritual renewal and rest commencing at sunset on Friday, terminating at nightfall on Saturday.
Shatnez	Shaatnez	Garments containing a forbidden mixture of wool and linen.
Shavuot		*Weeks.* One of three pilgrim festivals. Shavuot is celebrated in the summer, seven weeks after Pesach.
Shekhina		The divine presence.
Shema		Major Jewish prayer affirming belief in one God. The Shema is found in the Torah.
Shemot		*Names.* Seven holy names of God.
Shiva		Seven days of intense mourning following the burial of a close relation. During this period, all ordinary work is prohibited.
Shoah		*Desolation.* The suffering experienced by European Jews at the hands of the Nazis, including the systematic murder of six million Jews between 1933 and 1945.
Shofar		Ram's horn blown at the season of Rosh Hashanah.
Siddur		*Order.* Daily prayer book.
Simchat Torah		*Rejoicing of the law.* Festival celebrating the completion and recommencement of the cycle of the weekly Torah reading.

Judaism

PREFERRED FORM	MAIN VARIANTS	EXPLANATION
Sukkah	Sukkot (pl.)	*Tabernacle; booth.* A temporary dwelling used during Sukkot.
Sukkot		One of three biblical pilgrim festivals, Sukkot is celebrated in the Autumn.
Synagogue	Shul Bet Haknesset Bet Hamidrash	Building for Jewish public prayer, study and assembly.
Tallit	Tallith	*Prayer shawl.* Four-cornered garment with fringes.
Talmud		Mishnah and Gemara, collected together.
Tefillah	Tefila	*Self-judgement.* Jewish prayer and meditation.
Tefillin	Tephilin T'filin Phylacteries	Small leather boxes containing passages from the Torah, strapped on the forehead and arm for morning prayers on weekdays.
Tenakh	Tanakh	The collected 24 books of the Jewish Bible, comprising three sections: Torah, Nevi'im, and Ketuvim (Te;Na;Kh).
Teshuva		*Repentence.* Returning to God.
Tikkun Olam	Tikun	Care for the world and environment.
Torah		*Law; teaching.* The Five Books of Moses.
Tzedaka		*Righteousness.* An act of charity.
Tzizit	Tzittzit	Fringes on the corners of the Tallit. Also commonly refers to the fringed undervest worn by some Jewish males.
Yad		Hand-held pointer used in reading the Sefer Torah.
Yahrzeit		*Year-time.* Anniversary of a death.
Yeshiva		College for study of the Torah and Talmud.
Yiddish		Language used predominantly by Ashkenazim.
Yishuv		*Ingathering.* The Jewish community of Israel.
Yom Hashoah		Day to commemorate the Shoah.
Yom Kippur		*Day of Atonement.* Fast day occuring on the tenth day after Rosh Hashanah; a solemn day of Tefillah and Teshuva.
Zionism		Political movement securing the Jewish return to the land of Israel.

SIKHISM GLOSSARY

Sikh terms are drawn from the Punjabi language, and the versions below are based upon that language. Many of these terms will also be found in books on Hinduism and Buddhism but with somewhat different meanings. As with all transliterations, there are problems which are difficult to resolve. This is particularly true when moving from the Gurmukhi script which has an alphabet of 35 letters, to the Roman alphabet which has only 26 letters.

Names of persons and places are only included in this list if variant forms are commonly used.

PREFERRED FORM	MAIN VARIANTS	EXPLANATION
Akal Purakh		*The Eternal One.* A designation frequently used of God by Guru Nanak.
Akal Takht	Akal Takhat	*Throne of the Eternal; throne of the Timeless One.* Building facing the Golden Temple in Amritsar, where Sikhs gather for political purposes.
Akhand Path		Continuous reading of the Guru Granth Sahib from beginning to end.
Amrit		*Nectar.* Sanctified liquid made of sugar and water, used in initiation ceremonies.
Amrit ceremony	Amrit Sanskar Amrit Pahul Khande di Pahul Sometimes just 'Amrit' or 'Taking Amrit' ('Amrit Chhakna')	The Sikh rite of initiation into the Khalsa. 'Baptism' should not be used.
Anand karaj	Anand Sanskar	*Ceremony of bliss.* Wedding ceremony.
Ardas		*Prayer.* The formal prayer offered at most religious acts.
Baisakhi	Vaisakhi	A major Sikh festival celebrating the formation of the Khalsa, 1699 CE.
Bangla Sahib		The site of the martyrdom of Guru Har Krishan (Delhi).
Bhai Khanaya		A Sikh commended by Guru Gobind Singh for serving water to the enemy wounded.
Bhai Lalo		A humble carpenter who opened his house to Guru Nanak. The Guru preferred Bhai Lalo's simple food to the offerings of a local rich merchant.
Chanani	Chandni	Canopy over the scriptures, used as a mark of respect.

Sikhism

PREFERRED FORM	MAIN VARIANTS	EXPLANATION
Chauri	Chaur	Symbol of the authority of the Guru Granth Sahib. Fan waved over scriptures, made of yak hairs or nylon. It should not be called a 'fly whisk'.
Dasam Granth		Collection of compositions, some of which are attributed to the tenth Sikh Guru, compiled some years after his death.
Giani		A person learned in the Sikh scriptures.
Granthi		Reader of the Guru Granth Sahib, who officiates at ceremonies.
Gurbani	Bani, Vani	Divine word revealed by the Gurus. The Shabads contained in the Guru Granth Sahib.
Gurdwara	Gurudwara	Sikh place of worship. Literally the 'doorway to the Guru'.
Gurmat		*The Guru's guidance.*
Gurmukh		One who lives by the Guru's teaching.
Gurmukhi		*From the Guru's mouth.* Name given to the script in which the scriptures and the Punjabi language are written.
Gurpurb	Gurpurab	A Guru's anniversary (birth or death). Also used for other anniversaries, eg of the installation of the Adi Granth, 1604 CE.
Guru		Teacher. In Sikhism, the title of Guru is reserved for the ten human Gurus and the Guru Granth Sahib.
Guru Arjan		The fifth Guru who was the first Sikh martyr (1563-1606).
Guru Gobind Singh	Guru Govind Singh (Original name: Guru Gobind Rai)	Tenth Sikh Guru. It is important to note that the title 'Guru' must be used with all the Gurus' names. Sikhs usually use further terms of respect, eg Guru Gobind Singh Ji or Guru Nanak Dev Ji.
Guru Granth Sahib	Adi Granth (Granth' by itself should be avoided)	Primal collection of Sikh scriptures, compiled by Guru Arjan and given its final form by Guru Gobind Singh.
Guru Har Gobind	Guru Hargobind Guru Hargovind	Sixth Sikh Guru.
Guru Har Krishan Guru Harkishan	Guru Harkrishan	Eighth Sikh Guru.

SIKHISM

Sikhism

PREFERRED FORM	MAIN VARIANTS	EXPLANATION
Guru Nanak		The first Guru and the founder of the Sikh faith (1469-1539).
Guru Tegh Bahadur		The ninth Guru who was martyred for the principle of religious tolerance (1622-1675).
Haumai		*Egoism.* The major spiritual defect.
Hukam		*God's will.*
Hukam	Vak	Random reading taken for guidance from the Guru Granth Sahib.
Ik Onkar		*There is only One God.* The first phrase of the Mool Mantar. It is also used as a symbol to decorate Sikh objects.
Janamsakhi	Janam Sakhi	*Birth stories.* Hagiographic life stories of a Guru, especially Guru Nanak.
Japji Sahib		A morning prayer, composed by Guru Nanak, which forms the first chapter of the Guru Granth Sahib.
Jivan Mukt	Jivan Mukht	Enlightened while in the material body; a spiritually enlightened person, freed from worldly bonds.
Kachera		Traditional underwear/shorts. One of the five K's (see panj kakke).
Kakka	Singular of the Punjabi letter K (plural 'Kakke')	See panj kakke.
Kangha	Kanga	Comb worn in the hair. One of the five K's (see panj kakke).
Kara		Steel band worn on the right wrist. One of the five K's (see panj kakke).
Karah parshad	Karah Prasad	Sanctified food distributed at Sikh ceremonies.
Kaur		*Princess.* Name given to all Sikh females by Guru Gobind Singh (see Singh).
Kesh	Kes	Uncut hair. One of the five K's (see panj kakke).
Khalsa		*The community of the pure.* The Sikh community.
Khanda		Double-edged sword used in the initiation ceremony. Also used as the emblem on the Sikh flag.

Sikhism

PREFERRED FORM	MAIN VARIANTS	EXPLANATION
Kirat karna		Earning one's livelihood by one's own efforts.
Kirpan		Sword. One of the five K's (see panj kakke). 'Dagger' should be avoided.
Kirtan		Devotional singing of the compositions found in the Guru Granth Sahib.
Kirtan Sohila		A prayer said before retiring for sleep. It is also used at the cremation ceremony and when the Guru Granth Sahib is laid to rest.
Kurahit		Prohibitions, eg intoxicants.
Langar	Guru ka Langar	*Guru's kitchen.* The gurdwara dining hall and the food served in it.
Mela		*Fair.* Used of Sikh festivals which are not gurpurbs.
Manji	Manji Sahib	Small platform on which the scripture is placed.
Manmukh	Munmukh	Self-orientated (as opposed to gurmukh).
Mool Mantar	Mul Mantar	*Basic teaching; essential teaching.* The basic statement of belief at the beginning of the Guru Granth Sahib.
Nam Simran	Nam Simaran Naam Simran	Meditation on the divine name, using passages of scripture.
Nankana Sahib		Birthplace of Guru Nanak. Now in Pakistan.
Nishan Sahib		Sikh flag flown at gurdwaras.
Nit nem		The recitation of specified daily prayers.
Panj kakke		*The five K's.* The symbols of Sikhism worn by Sikhs.
Panj piare	Panj Pyare (other forms may also be found)	*The five beloved ones.* Those first initiated into the Khalsa; those who perform the rite today.
Panth		The Sikh community.
Patases	Patashas	Sugar bubbles or crystals used to prepare Amrit.
Punjab	Panjab	*Land of five rivers.* The area of India in which Sikhism originated.
Ragi		Sikh musician who sings compositions from the Guru Granth Sahib.

Sikhism

PREFERRED FORM	MAIN VARIANTS	EXPLANATION
Raheguru		*Wonderful Lord.* A Sikh name for God.
Rahit		Sikh obligations, eg to meditate on God.
Rahit Maryada	Rehat Maryada	Sikh Code of Discipline.
Sadhsangat	Sangat	Congregation or assembly of Sikhs.
Sewa	Seva	Service directed at the sadhsangat and gurdwara, but also to humanity in general.
Shabad	Sabad Shabd	*Word.* Hymn from the Guru Granth Sahib; the divine word.
Sikh		*Learner; disciple.* A person who believes in the ten Gurus and the Guru Granth Sahib, and who has no other religion.
Singh		*Lion.* Name adopted by Sikh males (see kaur).
Sis Ganj Sahib		The site of the martyrdom of Guru Tegh Bahadur (Delhi)
Vak	Vaak	A random reading taken for guidance from the Guru Granth Sahib.
Vand chhakna		Sharing one's time, talents and earnings with the less fortunate.